BOUNCING BACK FROM EXTINCTION

THE RETURN OF THE
MANATEE

TANYA DELLACCIO

PowerKiDS press™
New York

Published in 2018 by The Rosen Publishing Group, Inc.
29 East 21st Street, New York, NY 10010

First Edition

Editor: Theresa Morlock
Book Design: Reann Nye

Photo Credits: Cover Brian J. Skerry/National Geographic/Getty Images; pp. 4, 27, 28 Andrea Izzotti/ Shutterstock.com; p. 5 (Pyrenean ibex) dragoms/Moment Open/Getty Images; p. 5 (jaguar) Travel Stock/ Shutterstock.com; p. 5 (Arctic fox, hippopotamus) bikeriderlondon/Shutterstock.com; p. 5 (orangutan) Sergey Uryadnikov/Shutterstock.com; p. 5 (Wyoming toad) https://commons.wikimedia.org/wiki/ File:Bufo_baxteri-3.jpg; pp. 7, 10, 11, 15, 18, 29 Greg Amptman/Shutterstock.com; p. 8 Michael Rosebrock/Shutterstock.com; p. 9 Colors and shapes of underwater world/Moment/Getty Images; p. 12 Mike Korostelev www.mkorostelev.com/Moment Open/Getty Images; pp. 13, 24 Ethan Daniels/ Shutterstock.com; p. 14 Rich Carey/Shutterstock.com; p. 17 Photo Researchers/Science Source/ Getty Images; p. 19 Carol Grant/Moment Select/Getty Images; pp. 20, 30 A Cotton Photo/ Shutterstock.com; p. 21 Michael Nolan/robertharding/Getty Images; p. 23 James R.D. Scott/Moment/ Getty Images; p. 25 Jason Edwards/National Geographic Magazines/Getty Images; p. 26 Alex Couto/ Shutterstock.com.

Cataloging-in-Publication Data

Names: Dellaccio, Tanya.
Title: The return of the manatee / Tanya Dellaccio.
Description: New York : PowerKids Press, 2018. | Series: Bouncing back from extinction | Includes index.
Identifiers: ISBN 9781508156239 (pbk.) | ISBN 9781508156161 (library bound) | ISBN 9781508156048 (6 pack)
Subjects: LCSH: Manatees–Juvenile literature.
Classification: LCC QL737.S63 D45 2018 | DDC 599.55–dc23

Manufactured in the United States of America

CPSIA Compliance Information: Batch #BS17PK: For Further Information contact Rosen Publishing, New York, New York at 1-800-237-9932

CONTENTS

THE ROAD TO EXTINCTION

When Christopher Columbus first saw manatees in 1493, he thought they were mermaids! Manatees' large, graceful bodies can be seen slowly traveling through waters in many warm areas of the world. This marine animal faces many challenges to survive in its underwater **habitat**.

Due to hunting, slow **reproduction**, habitat loss, and human thoughtlessness, manatees are either endangered or threatened in many places.

Over the past several years, people have made efforts to **reverse** the manatee's road to extinction and improve the species' survival rate. Laws now make it illegal to hunt or harm manatees. Speed limits and guidelines for boaters also lower the risk of wounding the creatures.

Manatees live in shallow, slow-moving water.

CONSERVATION STATUS CHART

EXTINCT

Having no living members.

Pyrenean ibex

EXTINCT IN THE WILD

Living members only in captivity.

Wyoming toad

CRITICALLY ENDANGERED

At highest risk of becoming extinct.

Sumatran orangutan

ENDANGERED VULNERABLE

High risk of extinction in the wild.

hippopotamus

NEAR THREATENED

Likely to become endangered soon.

jaguar

LEAST CONCERN

Lowest risk of endangerment.

Arctic fox

THE MANATEE FAMILY

There are three species in the manatee family, each of which lives in different areas of the world. Amazonian manatees can be found in the Amazon River in South America. African manatees live in and around the west coast and rivers of Africa. The third, and best-known, species of manatee is the West Indian manatee. This species is found along the East Coast of North America, as well as Central and South America.

The West Indian manatee is well known because of its high risk of extinction and the successful efforts made to save its population. The species has become a symbol for **conservation** in the United States. Many groups provide people with information on ways to help it survive.

THE IUCN

The International Union for Conservation of Nature (IUCN) researches many species of animals. The group lists each species and subspecies according to its survival rate in the hope of conserving and increasing the populations. The West Indian manatee is now considered vulnerable.

The West Indian manatee was first listed as endangered in 1967. However, after conservation efforts and a large rise in population, the IUCN changed the West Indian manatee to vulnerable in 2016.

SLOW AND STEADY

Manatees are very slow creatures. Their unhurried, mild habits have earned them the nickname "sea cow." Manatees can weigh anywhere from 440 to 1,300 pounds (200 to 589.7 kg)! Their big bodies don't allow them to travel very fast. In fact, manatees often just float around alone or in pairs, not moving much at all. They usually swim about 5 miles (8 km) per hour. They can

BOATING DANGER

Around 30 percent of manatee deaths in Florida are caused by crashes with boats. Since manatees are such big creatures, it's difficult to avoid hitting them. In 2016, more than 100 manatees were killed by boats in Florida alone. Speed limit signs are often posted in areas where manatees live. You can find tips and tools to use when boating near manatees on the Florida Fish and Wildlife Conservation Commission website.

MANATEE ZONE

SLOW SPEED
MINIMUM WAKE

TO REPORT DAMAGED MARKERS: (866) 405-BUOY

swim up to 15 miles (24.1 km) per hour, but they're only able to do so for a short period of time.

Since manatees move so slowly as they float around in the water, boats can crash into them. Many areas now have laws to protect manatees from such accidents. Thanks to these laws, the rate of manatee deaths has decreased.

A BREATH OF FRESH AIR

When swimming, manatees need to breathe every five minutes or so. When resting, they can hold their breath for up to 20 minutes. Since manatees aren't able to breathe underwater like some marine animals, they often float at the surface of the water. This puts them at a higher risk of being hit by boats and other dangers such as getting caught in fishing nets.

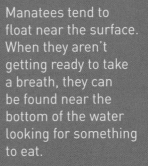

Manatees tend to float near the surface. When they aren't getting ready to take a breath, they can be found near the bottom of the water looking for something to eat.

A manatee is able to change its **buoyancy**, letting it float or sink to different depths in the water. To do this, they use their rib cage muscles to change the amount of air in their lungs. They use this trick to rise to the surface to breathe instead of spending energy swimming.

PLANT EATERS

In between breaths, manatees float around and look for food. Manatees spend about 10 to 12 hours sleeping and 8 hours eating every day. All manatees are herbivores, which means they only eat plants, such as sea grass and algae. They can eat up to 10 percent of their body weight in food in a single day! Although they look very round, manatees aren't fat. They actually don't have enough blubber, or fat, to keep them warm.

Manatees sometimes eat more than 100 pounds (45.4 kg) of food a day!

Manatees have many other adaptations that help them survive in the wild waters. Their teeth can become dull and worn down from biting through tough plants and accidentally chewing sand while they eat. However, they continue growing new teeth. A manatee can grow around 30 or more new teeth during its lifetime.

LOSING FOOD SOURCES

One of the biggest problems manatees face is the loss of their habitats. Scientists have observed that sea grass habitats are in danger. As sea grass is lost, manatees have a harder time finding food, making it more difficult for them to eat a healthy amount.

Sea grass is in danger for a few reasons. Pollution plays a big part in harming sea grass and ocean habitats around the world. It's important to be mindful of the

Even though food may sometimes be tough to find, manatees can search around the seafloor with their mouth. They're able to move their mouth and grab onto things in a way similar to how people use their fingers.

trash we produce and remember that it may damage animal habitats.

Changes in water temperature can also cause water plants to die. Many plants need specific temperatures to stay healthy. When temperatures are warmer or colder than usual, the plants can't survive.

WARM AND COZY

Temperature changes in a manatee's ecosystem can harm more than just the plants. Manatees need warm waters to keep a healthy body temperature. This is even more important for West Indian and African manatees because they live in salt water. Amazonian manatees live in the Amazon River, which is freshwater. The Amazon River is warm enough that the Amazonian manatees don't need to travel to search for warmer areas.

Finding warm water is more difficult during the winter. The Florida manatee, a subspecies of the West Indian manatee that lives mostly in Florida, faced a big population loss during a very cold winter in 2010. About 250 manatees died due to problems caused by the cold waters. Florida manatees sometimes travel to warmer waters during the winter.

MANATEE TRAVELS

Since the weather and temperature change with the seasons, Florida manatees tend to travel to warmer locations during the colder months of the year. Some Florida manatees have even been seen as far away as Texas! People have created safe spaces for manatees where boats aren't allowed during certain time periods. This gives manatees a safe place to rest until the weather warms up and they can return home.

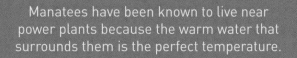

Manatees have been known to live near power plants because the warm water that surrounds them is the perfect temperature.

KEEPING WILDLIFE SAFE

The U.S. Fish and Wildlife Service is one of the biggest **advocates** for keeping animals and habitats safe and saving them from extinction. The service is part of the federal government. Its mission is to "conserve, protect, and **enhance** fish, wildlife, and plants and their habitats for the continuing benefit of the American people."

The U.S. Fish and Wildlife Service employs thousands of people throughout the United States.

An important part of manatee conservation is helping to save their habitat. The U.S. Fish and Wildlife Service works to help both manatees and the **environment** they live in.

They work together to research and learn about different species and habitats. These people have the common goal of conserving wildlife and the environments in which they live. Manatees have been an important topic of research and conservation for the U.S. Fish and Wildlife Service. The service's efforts have created a safer, more **sustainable** world for manatees to live in.

PROTECTING THE MANATEES

Hunting manatees is illegal in the United States. The laws that make it illegal have been largely proposed and managed by the U.S. Fish and Wildlife Service. The Marine Mammal Protection Act of 1972 punishes anyone who hunts or harms not only manatees, but any marine mammal in the United States. The Endangered Species Act of 1973 protects species that are endangered and the habitats in which they live from being harmed.

Both the Amazonian and African manatees are listed as vulnerable. There are fewer than 10,000 members of each species left in the wild.

THE AMAZONIAN MANATEE

The Amazonian manatee lives a somewhat unknown life. Since the waters they live in are often darker and harder to get to, gathering information on this species has proven difficult. The ICUN Red List lists this species of manatee as vulnerable because they're hunted and because **global warming** has caused changes to their habitat.

These laws have helped the manatee population in the United States grow. They've also helped the West Indian manatee bounce back from its road to extinction. Unfortunately, not all countries have similar laws and the Amazonian and African manatees are often in danger from poaching, or illegal hunting.

BABY MANATEES

The slow rate of manatee reproduction has also threatened their survival. In the wild, manatees can live for more than 50 years. A female can reproduce from about the time it's three or four years old and throughout its adult life. Unfortunately, the time it takes for a female to give birth to a calf, or baby, is very long. A mother manatee is pregnant for 12 to 14 months and usually waits at least 2 years before reproducing again.

This slow reproduction rate becomes a problem when deaths due to boating accidents and weather changes occur fairly frequently. Manatees are dying out faster than they're being born. Some female manatees can't reproduce because these factors have harmed their health.

A PEACEFUL LIFE

Adult manatees can be anywhere from 8 to 14 feet (2.4 to 4.3 m) long. Since their large bodies appear threatening to other animals, they don't have many predators. Manatees generally don't fight with each other, and even alligators have been known to move out of the way to let a manatee pass by.

A newborn manatee calf usually weighs around 60 pounds (27.2 kg) and is around 4 feet (1.2 m) long.

A SECOND CHANCE

Though manatees don't usually fight with each other, they're put in danger by outside forces. People are responsible for putting manatees at risk since boating accidents are one of the top reasons why the species is threatened. Rescue and rehabilitation efforts have been made to help restore the manatee population.

In some high-risk cases, manatees are given a tracking device before they're released back into the wild. This helps people observe their health and progress when they're back in their natural habitat.

The U.S. Fish and Wildlife Service created the Manatee Rescue, Rehabilitation, and Release Program to help keep up the population of the West Indian manatee. This program allows people to inform the service about manatees that appear to be injured. The program rescues the injured manatees and places them into a rehabilitation facility. A few zoos and aquariums throughout the United States provide these facilities. After a manatee is treated, it's released back into the wild.

BEING POLITE

A big part of making sure manatees don't become extinct is human awareness. There are many things you can do to help save the manatees. Being mindful of boating laws is an important step in keeping the species safe. Another is to learn about manatee refuges.

Seeing a manatee can be really interesting, but it's important to remember not to get too close. Manatees

Manatees can be very interesting animals, but when you're near one it's important to keep a safe distance and be aware of the rules set by experienced professionals.

are very gentle creatures. Some places even offer the opportunity to swim alongside them. However, touching a manatee can cause unnecessary anxiety to the animal and threaten its peaceful existence in the waters. The U.S. Fish and Wildlife Service's website provides a series of "Manatee Manners" videos that give in-depth instructions on how to handle an up-close manatee interaction.

BOUNCING BACK

As a whole, the West Indian manatee species is listed as vulnerable on the IUCN Red List as of 2016. This means conservation efforts have pulled it back from its road to extinction. It's gone from being listed as endangered to at risk of being endangered. The Florida manatee is now listed as threatened rather than endangered.

The fight to protect the gentle sea cow is ongoing.

Following specific laws and guidelines are key parts of the fight to keep the manatee a part of our water habitats. Research, rehabilitation, and conservation efforts by agencies and the general public have caused an increase in the manatee population around the world. By continuing these efforts, there's hope that the manatee will soon be thriving rather than threatened.

TIMELINE OF EVENTS

1966 Manatees are listed as an endangered species under the Endangered Species Preservation Act.

The Marine Mammal Protection Act makes it illegal to harm or kill any marine mammal in the United States. **1972**

1973 The Endangered Species Act is created. This act protects all species listed as endangered and provides conservation efforts to help them bounce back from extinction.

The Florida Manatee Sanctuary Act is put into place. This makes the entire state a refuge for manatees. **1978**

1980 The first recovery plan is created for West Indian manatees. It maps out ways in which the species could be restored.

About 250 manatees are found dead after temperatures in central-east and southwest Florida drop below normal. **2010**

2016 The U.S. Fish and Wildlife Service petitions to have the West Indian manatee downgraded from endangered to threatened.

Surveys conclude that there are at least 6,620 manatees living in Florida's waters. **2017**

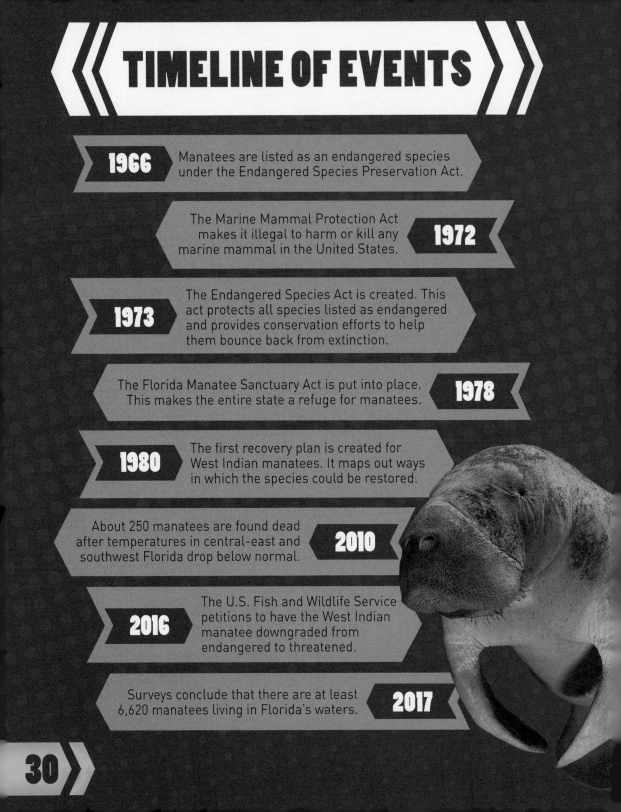

GLOSSARY

advocate: Someone who argues for or supports a cause or policy.

buoyancy: The ability to float or rise in water.

conservation: Efforts to care for the natural world.

enhance: To increase or improve the quality of something.

environment: The conditions that surround a living thing and affect the way it lives.

global warming: A gradual increase in how hot Earth is. It's believed to be caused by gases that are released when people burn fuels such as gasoline.

habitat: The natural home for plants, animals, and other living things.

reproduction: The process of having babies.

reverse: To turn in the opposite direction.

sustainable: Able to last a long time.

INDEX

WEBSITES

Due to the changing nature of Internet links, PowerKids Press has developed an online list of websites related to the subject of this book. This site is updated regularly. Please use this link to access the list: www.powerkidslinks.com/bbe/manatee